TRUE CRIME

CELEBRITY CASES

T. R. Thomas

TRUE CRIME

SADDLEBACK
EDUCATIONAL PUBLISHING
www.sdlback.com

ISBN-13: 978-1-59905-435-3
ISBN-10: 1-59905-435-3
eBook: 978-1-60291-761-3

18 17 16 15 14   6 7 8 9 10

Photos:
Anna Nicole Smith, Getty Images
Paris Hilton, Reuters/Corbis
Li'l Kim, Getty Images
O.J. Simpson, Reuters/Corbis
Martha Stewart, Reuters/Corbis

CONTENTS

INTRODUCTION

Celebrities are often treated differently than other people. People they don't know approach them. Fans ask for autographs and tell them how great they are. Some celebrities make millions of dollars.

There is a downside, though. *Paparazzi* chase celebrities for photographs. Tabloid newspapers run articles or photos that make them look bad. Stalkers sometimes hurt or even kill celebrities.

Celebrities are people just like everyone else. They have fears and feel stress and pressure. Sometimes, the stress can lead to crime. Some celebrities become criminals. Others become victims.

O.J. Simpson beat his wife. He may have killed her, too. O.J. was found innocent. Later, he went to jail for other crimes. Martha Stewart spent time in jail for lying. After that she was under house arrest.

Other celebrities have trouble with drugs and alcohol. River Phoenix, Robert Downey Jr., Paris Hilton, and Lindsay Lohan are examples.

Hip-hop artists have also had plenty of troubles. Tupac Shakur and Notorious B.I.G. died. Lil' Kim spent time in prison.

Anna Nicole Smith's case is still a mystery. Her 2007 death was called an accidental overdose. Some people think she may have been murdered.

It is true that fame has its rewards. But sometimes there is also a terrible price to pay.

DATAFILE

T I M E L I N E

June 12, 1994

Nicole Brown Simpson and Ron Goldman are murdered.

October 3, 1995

O.J. Simpson is found not guilty of murder at his criminal trial.

December 5, 2008

O.J. is sentenced to 33 years in prison for other crimes.

Where is Lovelock, Nevada?

KEY TERMS

decapitated—beheaded; head cut off

domestic violence—harming someone in the same family or home

plaintive—sad or mournful

possessive—wanting to keep another person all to yourself

prophetic—predicting the future

DID YOU KNOW?

After Nicole Brown Simpson's death, her sister Denise Brown established a foundation. Its motto is: "There is no excuse for abuse." The group's goal is to help end domestic violence.

O.J. SIMPSON

There was almost no traffic on the I-405 freeway in Los Angeles. This was unusual for a late afternoon in June. A white Ford Bronco traveled slowly down the freeway. It was going about 35 mph. A large group of police cars followed it.

About 20 news helicopters flew overhead. People lined up along the overpasses to watch. More than 95 million people watched on TV. Most TV stations stopped their regular shows to cover the chase. NBC even broke into its coverage of the NBA Finals.

O.J. Simpson is shown with his ex-wife, Nicole, and their children on March 16, 1994. Less than three months later, Nicole was murdered.

Al Cowlings was driving the white Bronco. Orenthal James "O.J." Simpson was in the passenger seat. O.J. had a gun to his own head. He was talking on his cell phone with an LAPD officer. Detective Tom Lange was trying to talk O.J. out of killing himself.

O.J., or "the Juice," was Al Cowlings' best friend. The two men were both from San Francisco. They had gone to high school and college together. They had both played pro football in the NFL. O.J. later went on to become a popular sportscaster.

June 17, 1994, was a very bad day for Simpson. The police charged him with two murders. His ex-wife, Nicole Brown Simpson, had been stabbed to death. Her friend, Ron Goldman, was also murdered. The police thought O.J. had killed them both in a fit of rage. They wanted him to turn himself in.

Finally, he did. The low-speed chase ended at his mansion. O.J. was arrested.

A Marriage Gone Sour

O.J. and Nicole met in June 1977. Beautiful, blonde Nicole was only 18 at the time. She worked as a waitress at a swank Beverly Hills nightclub. That is where they met. O.J. was 30. He was still married to his first wife, Marguerite. They had three kids. But that did not stop O.J. from dating other women. Later, he would cheat on Nicole, too.

O.J. and Marguerite got a divorce. O.J. and Nicole married in 1985. Later that year, they had a baby girl, Sydney. In 1988, they had a baby boy, Justin.

By then O.J. had retired from professional football. He was working as a sportscaster. He also acted in movies and did commercials. He was famous as the spokesman for Hertz car rentals.

O.J. and Nicole seemed to make a beautiful couple. But, their marriage was no bed of roses. O.J. was very *possessive* and jealous. He couldn't stand to think of his wife with another man.

He also had an explosive temper. Nicole was a victim of *domestic violence.* O.J. beat her and called her names. He tried to make her feel worthless. She had to call 911 on him several times. She wrote about it in her diary.

Eventually they divorced. O.J. continued to stalk his ex-wife. A week before her death, Nicole told a friend O.J. was going to kill her. She said he was going to get away with it. He was going to charm the world because he was O.J. Simpson. Later, Nicole's words seemed *prophetic.*

Last Day on Earth for Nicole and Ron

Sunday, June 12, 1994, was a beautiful day in Los Angeles. Nicole Brown Simpson woke up early. She fixed breakfast for her two kids. For Nicole, weekends meant doing fun things with the kids. At the time, Sydney was eight and Justin was six.

Nicole and her children lived in a comfortable condo. It was in Brentwood. Brentwood is a wealthy Los Angeles neighborhood.

They had a busy day planned. First Nicole was taking the kids out shopping. Sydney had a dance recital that afternoon. The little girl had practiced a lot. She was excited about her costumes.

Early in the afternoon, O.J. called Nicole from his car. They talked about Sydney's recital. O.J. was planning to attend. Nicole's parents and sisters would be there as well.

Later that afternoon, O.J. met everybody at the recital. He arrived a little late. Several people noticed that he did not say hello to Nicole.

Nicole and her family were going out to dinner afterward. O.J. was not invited. They were going to Mezzaluna. It was a nice restaurant in Brentwood. Nicole's friend Ron Goldman worked there as a waiter.

O.J. had to catch a late flight to Chicago that night. He said goodbye after the recital. Everyone else went to the restaurant. Ron Goldman greeted the Brown party when they arrived. They had a nice dinner. Afterward, Nicole's mother went home. She did not realize she had left her glasses behind.

Later, the glasses were found in front of the restaurant. Ron Goldman offered to take them to Nicole. He left the restaurant. It was the last time his coworkers saw him alive.

On Trial for Murder

Sometime between 10 and 11 p.m., neighbors heard Nicole's dog barking. It seemed very distressed. The dog was wailing *plaintively*. It was running around loose in Nicole's neighborhood. The dog had blood on its back paw. Several neighbors tried to help. They did not know who the dog belonged to. It led them back to Nicole's condo.

The neighbors found the bodies of Nicole and Ron at the condo. They had been stabbed numerous times. Nicole's throat was slashed. She was nearly *decapitated*. The police immediately suspected O.J. They called him. He flew home from Chicago.

O.J. was questioned and released. Several days later, police arrested the former football star at the end of the famous slow-speed chase. O.J. Simpson was charged with the murders.

People from all over the world followed the trial. There were new developments every day. The evidence included a bloody glove and a Bruno Magli shoe print. Kato Kaelin, O.J.'s houseguest, testified. O.J.'s limo driver also testified. Every piece of the puzzle was examined.

O.J.'s defense team included F. Lee Bailey, Johnnie Cochran, and Robert Shapiro. The high-powered lawyers established reasonable doubt. O.J. was found not guilty.

The victims' families took O.J. to civil court after that. They sued him for wrongful death. They won the case. The judge ordered O.J. Simpson to pay the Goldmans and Browns 33.5 million dollars. He paid very little of that.

CELEBRITY CASES

O.J. Simpson has led a troubled life since then. In September 2007, he was involved in an armed robbery. On December 5, 2008, he was sentenced to 33 years in prison. Today, he is serving his sentence at Lovelock Correctional Center in Lovelock, Nevada.

CHAPTER 2

MARTHA STEWART

DATAFILE

T I M E L I N E

August 3, 1941

Martha Kostyra is born in Jersey City, New Jersey.

October 19, 1999

Martha's media corporation goes public. She becomes a billionaire.

June 4, 2003

Martha is arrested for her crimes.

Where is Westport, Connecticut?

CELEBRITY CASES

DID YOU KNOW?

Martha Stewart worked as a model when she was young. She appeared in TV commercials for soap and shampoo. She was also in ads for Tareyton cigarettes. Their slogan was "I'd rather fight than switch." The ads showed people with fake black eyes.

MARTHA STEWART

Martha Stewart is one of the most powerful women in America. She is the head of a media *conglomerate*. She also has her own TV show. At one point, her magazine sold more than two million copies a month. In 2004, she went to prison. Her media empire took a hit but recovered.

Martha's crime was not a violent one. She was convicted of a *white-collar crime*. She owned stock in a company called ImClone. It made cancer drugs. One of its new drugs failed to get FDA approval. That meant ImClone couldn't sell the

Martha Stewart leaves a hearing at federal court in New York.

new drug. That caused its stock price to drop sharply.

Martha found out about the FDA's decision beforehand. ImClone founder Samuel Waksal was a family friend. He told Martha and others that the stock price would go down. This is called *insider trading*. It is against the law. Eventually Waksal was sentenced to seven years in prison.

Martha sold her ImClone stock after receiving Waksal's tip. It was the day before the FDA announcement. Later she lied about it to investigators. That's what got her in trouble.

Jersey Girl Makes It Big

Many people think Martha Stewart was born wealthy. She has that look and manner. Certainly, Martha is wealthy now. However, she started as a working-class girl from New Jersey.

Martha Kostyra was born in 1941 to Polish-American parents. Her father was a salesperson. Her mother was a teacher. The family lived in Nutley, New Jersey. Martha was the second of six kids. She was bright and ambitious. She studied hard and got straight A's.

Martha's father taught her about gardening. She also learned cooking, baking, and sewing from her mother. Their next-door neighbors were retired bakers. Martha learned even more about baking from them.

As a teen, she started making extra money modeling. Then she got a scholar-ship to Barnard. Barnard is a women's college in Manhattan. She continued modeling while in college.

In 1961, she married Andy Stewart. He was a law student at Yale. In 1965, they had a daughter, Alexis. She was their only child.

Around this time, Martha became a stockbroker. She was very successful. But in 1973 the economy was bad. Martha and Andy moved with Alexis to Westport, Connecticut. They bought an 1805 farmhouse. It needed a lot of work. During the *restoration*, Martha learned a lot. She became very good at making an old home look beautiful.

Martha Starts Her Empire

In 1976, Martha started a catering business. She worked out of her basement. Soon it became a huge success. She fixed fancy foods to take to people's parties. She also managed a gourmet food store that did very well.

Martha's husband Andy worked in book publishing. He became president of a big New York publishing company. Martha catered a book release party for her husband's firm. She met a man at the party who was very impressed with her food. He asked if she would write a cookbook. The result was Martha's bestseller, *Entertaining*. It was a smash hit. Martha was on her way.

After that, she published many more books. They were all about cooking and home decoration. Martha also wrote newspaper and magazine articles. She appeared on talk shows, including Oprah and Larry King. Soon, she became known as a domestic diva.

Martha and Andy divorced in 1989. Not long after that she started a magazine, *Martha Stewart Living*. Her TV shows began a few years later. Martha also has her own line of housewares at K-Mart and Macys. She has branched out in many areas. She owns a lot of real estate as well.

CELEBRITY CASES

In 1997, she *consolidated* all of her media assets. She combined all of her magazines, TV shows, and other deals. She put them under one umbrella company called Martha Stewart Living Omnimedia. She decided to sell shares in her company. This made Martha Stewart very rich.

Life After Prison

After the ImClone scandal, Martha went to prison in 2004. She spent five months at the Alderson Federal Prison Camp in West Virginia. After that, she was under house arrest. She had to wear an ankle bracelet.

Being in jail did not stop Martha from being a domestic diva. She was allowed to make a clay nativity scene while in jail. Her daughter Alexis visited her often. Martha was not allowed to have a computer in jail. However, she could write letters on a prison typewriter.

Once she got out of jail, it was business as usual for Martha. Once again, her empire is growing. Some people are already forgetting that Martha Stewart was ever in jail.

DATAFILE

T I M E L I N E

October 31, 1993

River Phoenix dies of a drug overdose at age 23.

April 1996

Police arrest Robert Downey Jr. for carrying heroin, cocaine, and an unloaded .357 Magnum gun.

June 5, 2007

Paris Hilton goes to jail for DUI in Lynwood, California.

Where is Lynwood, California?

K E Y   T E R M S

addiction—having a strong craving for something; needing to use something all the time

cocaine psychosis—seeing things that aren't there as a result of using cocaine

convulsions—uncontrollable spasms of the body

idolize—to adore or worship someone and fail to see his or her faults

socialite—a well-known, often wealthy person who attends lots of parties

DID YOU KNOW?

Age 27 has been unlucky for many celebrities. Quite a few stars have died at that age. Most died from drugs or alcohol. These celebrities include Jimi Hendrix, Janis Joplin, Brian Jones of the Rolling Stones, Kurt Cobain of Nirvana, Freaky Tah of Lost Boyz, Kristen Pfaff of Hole, and many others.

PARTYING CELEBRITIES

Often, young people think it is cool to party. It seems fun to try drugs and alcohol. But partying can easily get out of hand. Drugs are illegal. Using them is a crime. Alcohol and drugs can ruin your life.

Substance abuse problems can be even worse for celebrities. Famous people are *idolized*. Their celebrity status makes it easy to get drugs. Often they are under a lot of stress. Partying is part of the lifestyle.

Partying can seem glamorous in the beginning. But after a while it gets old. People who party too much aren't respected. Other people don't trust them. Their lives spiral out of control.

Substance abuse can even result in death. River Phoenix is a sad example. At age 23, he was very successful. The promising young actor had starred in a number of movies. He was also an animal rights activist and an outspoken vegetarian.

He was partying on Halloween in 1993. He was at the Viper Room. The Viper Room is a popular Los Angeles nightspot. He had done a "speedball." A speedball is a powerful mixture of speed and heroin. Soon after, he was not feeling well. He started having *convulsions* on the sidewalk. Not long after that, he was dead from drug overdose. The bright young star's life was snuffed out.

In and Out of Jail and Rehab

Robert Downey Sr. once told his son, "When the *ritual* becomes *habitual,* it's time to quit." In 1996, police arrested Robert Downey Jr. It was not the first, or last, time. But it may have been the only time he was ever arrested naked. The actor was driving his Porsche around Los Angeles. He had no clothes on. He was throwing imaginary rats out of the car. He was suffering from *cocaine psychosis.* He thought he needed to cleanse himself and his car. Another time, he woke up in a Malibu neighbor's house. He had wandered into their home. He thought it was his house. He passed out in a child's bed. The neighbors were shocked to find him there.

In a way, these stories seem somewhat funny. They are, however, very sad. Downey could have killed or harmed someone. His substance abuse cost him a lot. His wife and several girlfriends left him over it. His problems caused him to lose important movie roles. They also landed him in jail several times.

Finally, Robert Downey Jr. got his act together. He decided once and for all that it wasn't worth it. With lots of help, he broke free from the nightmare of *addiction*. He turned his life around.

Famous for Being Famous

Paris Hilton is a famous, blonde *socialite*. She is the great-granddaughter of Conrad Hilton. Conrad Hilton was very rich. He started the Hilton Hotel chain.

Paris has had several minor movie roles. These include *Zoolander* and *House of Wax*. She won a Teen Choice Award for "Best Scream" in *House of Wax*. She also has done some modeling. In one ad, she appeared nude. Her body was painted gold.

Heiress Paris Hilton leaves the Los Angeles Municipal Court May 4, 2007. Hilton was ordered to spend 45 days in jail for violating the terms of her probation for alcohol-related reckless driving.

CELEBRITY CASES

Mainly, Paris Hilton is famous for going to jail. Her trouble started off with a DUI. That means *driving under the influence* of alcohol. As a result, the court suspended her license. She continued to drive anyway. Police pulled her over for going 70 mph in a 35 mph zone. She was driving in the dark with her lights off.

The judge sentenced her to 45 days in jail. On June 5, 2007, she was locked up in an all-female jail in Lynwood, California.

A Child Star Gone Bad

As a child, Lindsay Lohan was a cute, freckle-faced redhead. She grew up to be a fiery bombshell. Today, she is better known for her partying than for her acting.

Lindsay started off modeling when she was little. She modeled for companies like Calvin Klein and Abercrombie Kids. Then she moved up to TV commercials. She did a commercial for Jell-O with Bill Cosby. When she was 12, she won her first starring movie role in *The Parent Trap*.

As a teen she started appearing in popular movies like *Mean Girls*. Mattel made a Lindsay Lohan doll. She began recording music, too.

While she was still a teenager she got into alcohol and cocaine. In November 2007, Lindsay pleaded no contest to drunk driving. She spent 84 minutes in jail in Lynwood, California. It was the same jail Paris Hilton was sent to earlier that year.

CHAPTER 4

HIP-HOP TURF WARS

DATAFILE

TIMELINE

September 13, 1996

Tupac Shakur, 25, dies of gunshot wounds in Las Vegas.

March 9, 1997

The Notorious B.I.G., 24, dies of gunshot wounds in Los Angeles.

July 2005

Lil' Kim is sentenced to a year and a day in prison for lying about a shooting.

Where is Brooklyn, New York?

K E Y   T E R M S

iconic—relating to an object that symbolizes or means something

internship—a learning program involving hands-on work at a company, usually for no pay

retaliation—getting even for something

sporadic—happening occasionally

truce—an agreement not to fight anymore

DID YOU KNOW?

Sean "Diddy" Combs dated actress Jennifer Lopez for several years. J.Lo and Sean, who was then known as Puff Daddy, split in early 2001. J.Lo is now the richest Latina in Hollywood.

HIP-HOP TURF WARS

During the 1990s, East Coast hip-hop artists were at war with their West Coast rivals. At first, it was a war of words. In the mid-1990s, things got violent.

Two famous rappers died in an eerily similar way. Both were gunned down while sitting in their cars. Each was rushed to the hospital by his friends. Christopher "The Notorious B.I.G." Wallace died on the way to the hospital. Tupac Shakur held on for six days. The shootings happened several months apart.

CELEBRITY CASES

Biggie and Tupac were both from New York. Biggie was born in Brooklyn. Tupac was born in East Harlem. Shakur later moved with his family to the San Francisco Bay Area. He was associated with the West Coast rappers.

Shakur's label was Death Row Records. Suge Knight and Dr. Dre headed the Los Angeles-based record label. Its logo was a black man strapped to an electric chair. The label went bankrupt in 2009. The company's belongings were sold at auction. Its *iconic* electric chair was the hottest item. It sold for $2,500.

Biggie was with Sean "Diddy" Combs' recording company, Bad Boy Records. It was in New York. Combs had been an executive with Uptown Records before that. He had worked his way up from a non-paying *internship*. In 1993, he was fired from Uptown. He started Bad Boy

Records. Clive Davis, head of Arista Records, knew Combs and believed in him. He helped pay for the new startup.

Combs took some up-and-coming acts with him to the new label. Biggie was one of them. Craig Mack was another. Mack had a big hit with "Flava in Ya Ear." It went gold. Soon after that, Biggie released his *Ready to Die* album. It went multi-platinum. These successes helped Bad Boy Records get off to a good start.

New York was starting to take some of the spotlight. The Los Angeles crew was not happy about it.

The Spark Is Ignited

Hip-hop got its start in the 1970s in New York. That's where hip-hop music and culture began. In the late 1980s and early 1990s, West Coast rappers were very popular. Early West Coast hip-hop stars included Ice-T, MC Hammer, N.W.A., and The D.O.C. Dr. Dre and Snoop Dogg came a little later. Both were with Death Row Records.

Death Row was going strong in the early 1990s. The labels and artists were making a lot of money. The West Coast rappers were on top. But tempers flared when Sean "Diddy" Combs' East Coast crew started making waves. East Coast rapper Tim Dog released a song that disrespected Compton, California. That is probably what started the problems.

The feud got worse. In 1995, Death Row head Suge Knight criticized Sean Combs at the Source Awards. Knight suggested that new artists looking for a label should come to Death Row. He hinted they would get much better treatment than at Bad Boy Records.

In 1996, Tha Dogg Pound came out with a video. It showed New York skyscrapers being knocked over. Tha Dogg Pound was a Death Row act. In *retaliation*, some East Coast rappers put out a video of their own. It showed Tha Dogg Pound being thrown off the Queensboro Bridge.

After Biggie and Tupac were killed, a *truce* was called. Nation of Islam leader Louis Farrakhan called a number of hip-hop artists together. They agreed to stop the fighting. There was still *sporadic* violence after that. For the most part the fighting was over.

Lil' Kim and Junior M.A.F.I.A.

Lil' Kim, born Kimberly Denise Jones, is a rapper from Brooklyn. She was discovered by Biggie. Both were from the Bedford-Stuyvesant area of Brooklyn. "Bed-Stuy" is the home of many well-known hip-hop

Rapper Lil' Kim, whose real name is Kimberly Jones, arrives at court for her sentencing July 6, 2005, in New York City.

artists. They include Aaliyah, Jay-Z, Big Daddy Kane, Mos Def, Fabolous, and GZA.

Back then, Lil' Kim was part of a group called Junior M.A.F.I.A. Biggie had helped the group get off to a good start. He and Lil' Kim were close. She was the only female in his posse. That is how she got the nickname "Queen Bee." Lil' Kim went solo after Junior M.A.F.I.A. She had several platinum albums. She's known for her skimpy outfits and raunchy lyrics.

In 2001, she teamed up with several other female performers. They remade the 1974 Labelle hit "Lady Marmalade." The song was featured in the hit movie *Moulin Rouge.* It became a smash hit. It won a Grammy.

In 2005, Lil' Kim went to prison for lying to a grand jury about a shooting. The gun battle happened in 2001 outside radio station WQHT-FM. Lil' Kim's group ran into rival rappers Capone-N-Noreaga. In their song "Bang, Bang," rival Foxy Brown criticized Lil' Kim's music. The two groups argued. Gunfire broke out. One man was injured. Lil' Kim's friends Damion Butler and Suif Jackson later pleaded guilty to gun charges.

Lil' Kim told the grand jury she had not seen Butler and Jackson there that day. However, photographs taken at the scene proved she had. She admitted to lying to protect her friends.

"At the time I thought it was the right thing to do," she told the judge. "But I now know it was wrong."

DATAFILE

T I M E L I N E

November 28, 1967

Vickie Lynn Hogan is born in Harris County, Texas.

February 8, 2007

Anna Nicole Smith, 39, dies at a Florida hotel.

March 2009

Howard K. Stern and two doctors are arrested for having given Anna prescription drugs.

Where is Hollywood, Florida?

CELEBRITY CASES

K E Y   T E R M S

custody—the right to have a child live with you

despondent—feeling very sad or hopeless

entitled—having the right to something

heirs—the people who legally get someone's money after the person dies

paternity—fatherhood

DID YOU KNOW?

The NBC soap opera *Passions* ran from 1999 through 2007. The show was about the lives of people in a small New England town. One character was a spoof of Anna Nicole Smith. The character's name was Hannah Nicola Smythe. Suzanne Friedline played her.

ANNA NICOLE SMITH

Actress and model Anna Nicole Smith died in February 2007. She was found dead in her hotel room in Hollywood, Florida. The coroner listed the cause of death as accidental overdose. Some people think it may have been murder. Her life was full of drama. Her death has brought even more drama.

An Ongoing Legal Battle

Anna married an 89-year-old man when she was only 26. She was working at a strip club in Houston when they met.

Anna Nicole Smith departs with her attorney, Howard Stern, at the U.S. Supreme Court February 28, 2006. Smith was involved in a legal case before the court regarding the estate of her late husband, Texas oilman J. Howard Marshall II.

Anna claimed she loved the elderly man. Many people thought she married him for his money. Oil billionaire J. Howard Marshall liked to give Anna expensive gifts. He died just 13 months after they were married. He left Anna out of his will.

She believed she was *entitled* to half of his $1.6 billion estate. She went to court. Currently, the case is still in court. Anna Nicole Smith is dead. Her *heirs* will get the money if her side wins.

Anna gave birth to a baby daughter a few months before she died. Dannielynn Hope Marshall Birkhead was born September 7, 2006. Howard K. Stern was listed as the father. He was Anna's lawyer and live-in partner.

Several other men also claimed to be the father. *Paternity* testing in April 2007 proved Larry Birkhead was the father. The Los Angeles photographer had dated

Anna Nicole. He fought and won *custody* of her baby after she died.

Texas Blues

Anna Nicole Smith led a troubled life. She was born Vickie Lynn Hogan in Texas in 1967. Her mother was 16 when Vickie was born. Her parents divorced when she was a baby. Her mother and an aunt raised her.

Her mother, Virgie, was a police officer for 28 years. Virgie later married Donald Hart. Vickie Hogan changed her name to Nikki Hart. Later, her mother divorced and remarried several more times.

Anna's father, Donald Hogan, had several more kids. One of them was Donna Hogan. Donna later wrote a book about Anna. It was called *Train Wreck: The Life and Death of Anna Nicole Smith*.

Anna dropped out of high school as a sophomore. She worked as a waitress at

Jim's Krispy Fried Chicken. She met her first husband there. Billy Wayne Smith was a fry cook at Jim's. Anna married him when she was 17 and he was 16.

In 1986, Anna gave birth to a baby boy. His name was Daniel Wayne Smith. In 1987, Anna and her husband Billy separated. She moved to Houston with Daniel. She divorced Billy in 1993. She kept his last name.

Anna found a job at Wal-Mart in Houston. Later, she worked as a server at Red Lobster. In 1991, she became a stripper. She wanted to improve herself. She took modeling and voice lessons. Then she tried out for *Playboy* magazine and made it.

A Taste of Stardom

Being in *Playboy* boosted Anna's career. She was heavier than most *Playboy* models. However, she soon became a favorite. In

CELEBRITY CASES

March 1992, Hugh Hefner put her on the cover. She went by the name of Vickie Smith at that time. In 1993, she was Playmate of the Year. By then she was called Anna Nicole Smith.

New York magazine also put Anna on its cover. They used an unflattering photo taken as a joke. They titled the issue "White Trash Nation." Anna was squatting in white cowboy boots and eating chips. She sued the magazine.

Anna looked like Jayne Mansfield. Jayne was a blonde bombshell from the 1950s. She had been in *Playboy* in 1955. Anna was chosen to model Guess jeans. She was photographed posing like Jayne. Anna was also often compared to Marilyn Monroe. Marilyn was a famous actress, model, and singer. Marilyn died young.

Soon Anna was appearing in movies. In 1994, she had a bit part in *The Hudsucker*

Proxy. Later that year, she appeared in *Naked Gun 33-1/3: The Final Insult*. Her first starring role, in 1995, was in *To the Limit*. In 2002, she starred in her own reality show. *The Anna Nicole Show* took off with a bang. But it lost viewers quickly. It was canceled in February 2004.

Anna's legal battles continued. She also gained weight. At one point she was over 200 pounds. But then she lost a reported 69 pounds using TrimSpa. She became a spokeswoman for the company.

Anna's Tragic End

In September 2006, Anna was in the Bahamas. She had just given birth to her daughter. Daniel Smith, her 20-year-old son, came to the hospital to visit. Anna and Daniel had always been very close.

Daniel arrived on September 9. Early in the morning of September 10, he was seen checking on his mother. When Anna woke at 9:38, her beloved son was dead. He had died of a reaction from several prescription drugs.

Anna was *despondent*. Daniel had been the most important person in her life. At his funeral, she even tried to climb into the coffin with him. Her new baby daughter was the only thing keeping her going.

On February 8, 2007, Anna died too. Her death was very similar to Daniel's. They both died from a combination of prescription drugs. There were 11 different drugs in Anna's body when she died. None of them were prescribed for her. Eight were prescribed for Howard K. Stern.

In March 2009, Stern was arrested. He was charged with giving Anna the drugs that killed her. Two doctors were also charged for providing the prescriptions. Was Anna's death an accident or not? We may never know for sure.

GLOSSARY

addiction—having a strong craving for something; needing to use it all the time

cocaine psychosis—seeing things that aren't there as a result of using cocaine

conglomerate—a large corporation made up of a number of smaller companies

consolidate—to bring together into a single whole

convulsions—uncontrollable spasms of the body

custody—the right to have a child live with you

decapitated—beheaded; head cut off

despondent—feeling very sad or hopeless

domestic violence—harming someone in the same family or home

entitled—having the right to something

heirs—the people who legally get someone's money after the person dies

GLOSSARY

iconic—relating to an object that symbolizes or means something

idolize—to adore or worship someone and fail to see his or her faults

insider trading—illegally buying or selling stocks based on information that's not public

internship—a learning program involving hands-on work at a company, usually for no pay

paternity—fatherhood

plaintive—sad or mournful

possessive—wanting to keep another person all to yourself

prophetic—predicting the future

restoration—fixing up an old house so it is like new

retaliation—getting even for something

socialite—a well-known, often wealthy person who attends lots of parties

sporadic—happening occasionally

truce—an agreement not to fight anymore

white-collar crime—a nonviolent crime committed by a businessperson

INDEX

INDEX